Sex Injuries

By Redeeming Features

William Cornelius Harris Publishing

In collaboration

with

London Poetry Books

ISBN 978-1-911232-62-9

William Young Harris

34 Birchwood Close, Bordesley Road SM4 5N

London Poetry Books

Thank you to Levi Zerf, The Local, Pat Flowers, Keith Bray, Jason Why, Rich Bliss, Loz Vegas, Nouveau Bleach, Cable Street Beat, the Kilndown crew, The TWP, 108 Tattoo Shop, The Pole Hill Crew, Soft Play, Word Up Tunbridge Wells, the POW crew, Hedge Child, Roddy Moreno, PISSKRIEG, South London Wing Chun, Tim Wells, Hypermediaevents, Alex Wilding, Ollie, Attila the Stockbroker, John and Sarah from Overdrive Studios and Sam Stains. Big up Riot Act in Bristol.

In memory of Stefan

Cover artwork by HE Creative.

Logo Design by Jack Donovan

redeemingfeaturespoetry@yahoo.com

@redeemingf

Asymptomatic Super Gonorrhoea

Asymptomatic super gonorrhoea
They had no fucking idea
In the front, the mouth and the rear
Nobody was safe around here

Some people in Leeds
Spread their seeds
Did their deeds
And were brought to their knees

Not enough antibiotics
They're not as fun as narcotics
But you have to take them once you've got it
Or you'll find you have no way to stop it

Asymptomatic super gonorrhoea
A new beast was born. Oh shit. Oh dear.
Woe to you oh St. Leonards -on-sea
The devil sends the STD
With wrath
It tickles you more than a cough
Get yourself checked
Or you may regret
A young man's death
Roger McGough

Whether we're tall or short
We could all get caught
Look at what all the bonking brought
Don't tune into the latest transmission
You'll find you'll regret this decision
Stop the Madness. Fallout.
Call out.
Cock Lockdown
Dad brown
Calm it down
Ladies and boys
Stop sharing sex toys
All over town

Asymptomatic super gonorrhoea
You've got it but you think you're in the clear
Not all heroes wear jonnies
Wrong step
Patients
All shapes and sizes
Like 2 Ronnies
You shouldn't mix the pills with beer
This ain't any old mere
Ailment
Unstoppable freight train. 6 o'clock.
Up with the cock-rot
Judge Dreading the results. Derailment.

My mate was said to be patient zero
The stuff of legend, it rose again like emperor Nero
He ticked the stigma boxes
Like crack foxes
Playing bingo
And took the rumours like a hero

Asymptomatic super gonorrhoea
I'll talk about it all night, chew off your ear
Whether we're straight or gay or queer
It was an age of constant fear
Passing it around Blackpool pier to peer
Take the pills and stay off the gear
Asymptomatic super gonorrhoea

Banned From the Hippy Market

Banned from the hippy market
The poetry was too anarchic
Banned from the hippy market
Because I wasn't on a magic carpet
If I drove a hybrid, I would park it
Obscenity triggers. Click. Spark it.

I was jumping like Mario fighting Bowsers
They did Reiki and had parachute trousers
I offended some hippy ladies in blouses
They didn't think I was safe as houses
It shocked, appalled and caused fear
When I did a poem about diarrhoea

The market couldn't feature Redeeming
For fear of shit stains and of cleaning
The yoga teachers didn't like Redeeming Features
I didn't sell crystals or organic peaches
They don't care for vulgar speeches
But this is where the cult leader teaches

Banned from the hippy market
Namaste
I never planned on spitting there
All day
They said they only wanted Vipassana boys
Not people like me who make too much noise
They don't like the bars I choose

And they don't like me because I wear shoes
The hippies kicked me off mid-set
I don't listen to Psytrance or do ket
Maybe I'm making a thing of it
And really they just thought I was shit

Redeeming Features banned from the mic
Banned from the mic for talking shite
Redeeming Features on your bike
Redeeming Features take a hike
Until your features are out of site

Everyone Got Scabies

Everyone got scabies
Better that than rabies
Not so tiny mites
Bigger than stalactites
Alcatraz scaly breakouts
Fingernail rake outs
Midnight promethazine take-out
Skin drive-through
Drives you
Insane
Stuck here in the slow pain
The slow pain but with no gain

Shivery
Quivery
Pursuing recovery
Pesky critters
Unwanted body temple
Not so sweet home-sitters
Itchy shitters
Too much more than a little bitters

Everyone got scabies
The adults and the babies
Give us a miracle please
Or move me to the Maldives
It was in-between the fingers

It won't go it just lingers
Little hungry mingers
Mighty. Shitey. Spitey. Bitey.
Thought you saw em. Loosing sighty.
Is there a magic potion
Not just creams and lotion
Frequent scratching motion
Comes in waves like the ocean

Everyone got scabies
Rashes on the dailies
You can try rubbing bay leaves
Because you don't have to pay for these
Knock yourself out with Bailey's
Irish nightcap? Yes please
It makes your muscles seize
It don't come back like Herpes
You can't run it off doing burpees

Everyone got scabies
All the men and ladies
Itty bitty nitties
Infected all the hippies
Pissed-off angry crusties
Covered in scabies. Trust me.
The summer can get dusty
It's worse with scabies. Must be.

Eggs beneath the skin, see
I knew that you would agree
It’s not a nice disease
Everyone got scabies

Speeding International

Speeding international
No it wasn't rational
I spent too much cash n' all
On the way to Portugal
The roads are big enough for two
My amiga, the motor, plus me, yours you
She was the brains and I was the hassle
She was the pulse and I was the vessel

On the highways of Espanyola
Going so fast they couldn't have caught ya
In the back of an old transporter
Like Lou Reed
Agreed
Too much speed
Indeed

Fuck this
Ray Davies
Stooped so low lalala la lola
Livin' la vida loca
She was into martial arts
Vegetables and climbing walls
Coolant reservoir overflow
Gonna blow
Like red, white and blue-ball waterfalls

Over done it paces
Not serving aces
Too fast. Loaded-up whip.
Pain in the hip
Andy Murray
Mad dash
Fuel Splash
In a hurry
I should've known
Engine almost blown
Over heating
Foreign greeting
Like I'm late for a meeting
My presence was fleeting

The bank broke ya
Ringed out and choked ya
To be Frank though
Francisco
The stockbroker
Face like playing poker
Paring
Blaring
Lady Gaga
Roadside party mardi grada'

Breakdown
Like Hatebreed
Poor show

No
It's not what you need
Broke the law like the League
Anti going nowhere
Don't care

I had doubt
Then found out
Two long months on
That I got it wrong
A letter in the post
From a far-off coast
Said I had to pay the most
To my former host
Far too many kilometres
Can't lie. Sky high.
Engine thermometers
The price to pay was off the chart
Near miss, take piss, this is
As close as I've got to making fine art

I slipped and fell then dropped the ball
Ran and ran then hit the wall
It's not clever and big, it's small
Speeding International

Ballbag

One Ball. Two ball. Three ball. Shit.
This inflamed ball makes me feel sick
Earlier on there were just two
Now there's a third one hanging off of you

One ball. Two ball. Three ball. Ow.
There's a new ball there, but how?
Before there were two but there's three now
It feels like I've been kicked down there somehow

One Ball. Two ball. Three ball. Drain.
It needs lancing to ease the pain
It feels like it's gonna blow
It makes me walk all stooped and slow

Ball bag. Bad sag. Dangle sack.
It feels like my balls have had a smack
Swelled up pustules all pulsating
Gives me cramps like I'm menstruating

Bruising. Losing. Seething pain.
I can't walk straight. What a shame.
I cannot stride and stand up tall
Because I've grown an extra ball
It's causing me anxiety
There's a third ball inside of me

How does it feel?
It feels unreal
Like a rolling tombstone
The first two ain't alone
Number three's got a new home
It's painful to bone
Always beware
Cancer scare
Pull back your rugs
And check your spuds

Fluid oedema
Seepage cleaner
Simply the worst, taken a Turner Teena
Like a pendulous bully but meaner
Gives me nightmares, horror dreamer

Ball bag. Ball bag. One, two, three.
It feels uncomfortable when I wee
Cut it out and let me be
Take this new ball away somewhere I can't see

Semi-Skilled Hard Landscaping Labourer

I'm Redeeming Features and I dig holes
I don't want to brag but I out-dig the moles
On a good day I'm as quick as the Poles
Unleashing anger like raging hot coals
Give me a shovel and I'm hunting for souls
It beats digging myself a hole on the dole

Disassociation. Excavation.
Rave digging, DLA bidding.
Lack of brain power. Who am I kidding?
Poor decision. Full on Collision.
Rolling dicey. Icey road. Unkind.
Nothing left to find inside my mind. Skidding.

I dig the hole fast so I don't get the sack
Or end up in trouble like Stanley Yelnats
Unearthing pottery and ancient scrolls
There's no reason to have any other goals
Tunnelling as man and boy. Horsepower and foal.
Breaking my back is my favourite job role
Paying the price like French motorway tolls
I'm Redeeming Features and I dig holes

Mullet Slugs

Slugs in the mullet
Little hole they dug it
On the locks they tug
It's a nest for a bug
Thug
Slimey
Grimey
Bad timey
Not 1 but 2. Blimey.

Slugs in the barnet
They don't cause harm
It seems I've found a home grown
Unknown
Hitch hiker
Smells like shyster

Worked in grime
Rings out black
In the fuck it bucket
Slosh
Gosh
He held on through the mosh
Found him, how rude
I'm screwed
Should've had a wash

Slugs built themselves a crusty shack
Grimm like brothers
Dead like the others
Slipped out in the covers
I nurtured them like mothers

Slugs in the hair do
Didn't flush ‘em down the loo
Long drop
Need chop
Crop
Smallest you ever saw
Wriggling along the floor

Cement dust
Busting out
A tiny dead slug in your hair
Is enough to scar most into a cut
So shut the case
And clip off the waste
How many other bugs squidged into a paste
Were crammed inside there
Worked into my hair
No I did not care
Till I got 2 in there

Inside your socks your pants and your frocks
From the hippy site to the tower blocks
Don't comb your hair you’re in for some shocks
They hide in your mop, your shoes and your rugs

Grievous
Devious,
Make me want to leavious,
Like tiny little thievious
Or poltergeist like Peevious
You should never trusty
My brushing skills are rusty
Dusty
Crusty
Mullet slugs

My picture was in the Daily Mail

My picture was in the Daily Mail
Now they can never say that I fail
It was one of a few old tales
That left me restricted to bail

Redeeming featured in the Daily
So sit down and let me tell thee
It was a dark stormy night. Howling gale.
The photo made me look shady
And they didn't even pay me
They crept up behind me
Blindly
On my non-existent crime spree

I was snapped and put in a tabloid
It can make you paranoid
When you're being apprehended
Though you never even defended
It was 2013 at the G8
The image tried to recreate
But the real incident
Was not so militant

They stuck my photo in the Daily
After the Met knocked down that lady
Then they tried to frame me
But the photo came out grainy

My pic got in the Daily
Magistrate not the Old Bailey
Although they judge and doubt your face
The old bill didn't have a case
Assault of the Police that never occurred
The evidence showed this was absurd

In the aftermath of such court case misdemeanours
Barristers want you to take the Met to the cleaners
I declined after giving the option some thought
I didn't want to have to spend another day in court
So be careful young 'erberts when you're out on weekend capers
You might find yourself in a cell or featured in the papers

Heart FM

Through the days and up all night
Shopping centre and building site
The constant playing radio station
Rejoices in the celebration
Of the same repeating 20 songs
Once upon a time they were number ones
They play them until our brains are dust
In Heart FM we put our trust

Heart FM all day long
Why would we need a different song
Heart FM constant play
Heart FM Groundhog day
Beating hearts
Top 10 charts
Like playing darts
Treble 20? No thanks. Repeat.
They always sing from the same hymn sheet

It makes my mind feel toxic
Roxette
Listen to your heart when he's calling to you
There's nothing I'd like less to do
Total eclipse of the brain fart
Internal organ body part
This endless repetition is rough
Disc jockey play some other stuff

Heart FM show us some compassion
You're playing these songs more than our ration
This radio station
Requires self-medication
Heart FM you're driving me away from sobriety
Please just give us at least some variety
Is hearing this jumping record tough?
Me too
Like T2
'I'm heartbroken without your love
I'm heartbroken 'cause I've had enough
I'm heartbroken
I don't know what to say
I've never felt this way'

Please start playing some different artists
Oh no
The radio
Is gaining influence over me
Paying the penalty
Like Southgate
Frustrate
Mind pollution
45 revolution
Grab ya' catapult
This is revolt
-ing like the Chartists

It sends you more crazy than loony toons
5 LPs or 60 tunes
Is too many songs for me and youse
You don't get to pick and choose
Heart FM is the drug that the bosses use
Mind numbing is what Heart FM is for
Like Soma or 1984
Brave new station what do you think?
Heart FM pushes your mind to the brink

Cardiology
Thought criminology
Brain wash psychology
No apology
For this last resort
Report
Pathology
Longing for silence
Violence
In the mind
Maybe we're better off deaf than blind
Attention workers all aboard
This one-way trip to the psyche ward

Emulate the same behaviour
Bad reception is our only saviour
Vascular sanity test
Give this cardiac a rest

Ear worm
Brain churn
Day in day out
What's this about?
I know the lyrics
I've gone from cynic
To enthusiast
And I'm gassed
When for the 50th time that day I hear Bieber
I've spent so long in the place
Now I’m a Belieber

These days I find when I'm in the car
I don't have to travel far
Before I cave and switch the station
To the favourite channel of the nation
The familiarity does something for me
When the roads are bleak and stormy
You could say it's grown on me a tad
Since I stopped being such an angry lad
It no longer seems to make me mad
Heart FM you're not so bad

Portuguese Mountain Ben

His name's Ben
One of the Portuguese mountain men
Tattooed attitude
And in the sunshine, semi-nude
Top bloke never rude
He spent the 90s avoiding pen
He moved here from the Scottish fens
And achieved high levels of zen
He's been at it since god knows when
But his neighbour is shouting at him again

Ben travelled long and far
Across miles of gravel and tar
To open a biker bar
But there's always one you know
Who has to cause aggro
And won't let things go

Co-habitants'
Arms are flailing
Pissed off and wailing
Harpoon high noon
Attack. Endangered. Early afternoon.
Faces slinging. War cry singing.
1pm. Kicked off too soon.
Like a cartoon
But Ben 10 is called Ben 10

Because Ben's got 10 out of 10 zen
Does Ben
He wanted to retire like Sven Yon Eriksson
But matey
From the front gate
Three doors up
Has come for a punch up
And is
Screaming at him on his porch
One man angry mob pitch fork and torch

Livewire
Medieval-style funeral pyre
Please Sire
More leary than Danny Dyer's
Noughties roles
No pleasantry, unnecessary
Conflict beneath scaffolding poles

Verbal assassin in red hot pursuit
High tailing
Got to stand your ground
No chance of bailing
Local short fuse out for an impaling
Damaged filament
Uncalled for argument
More slander than sitting in parliament
Ticking time bomb
Where's your Chi – gone?

Oh no
He's gonna blow
Stooped so low
Can't let go
Won't be long
You're in the wrong
Leave us be
Like Bruce Lee
Be like water
That's what you outta'
Do
Think about Buddha. What he said was true.
And maybe you too
Should do what he would do
I can't go on with or without ya'
I thought you'd calm down but I started to doubt ya
It's a beautiful day
But you let it get away
You had to come and have your pissed off say

Ferocious Viking style raiding
Like Iron Maiden
Ran to the hills to get some silence
Not to partake in mountain top violence
Can't you see this is Ben's home
So go home and leave Ben alone
No you can't come in the bar
The bridges have all been burnt to char
A sad and sorry state of affairs
When cocaine leads to threatening glares

A lost soul left to wander free
Starting grief with you and me
He didn't understand, we didn't think he would
Here we are, there goes the neighbourhood

What happens in the mountains stays in the hills
Too much speed and too many pills
Drowning in fury like a fish without gills
Leaves a sour taste. Drinking urine like ‘Bear Grills’
Consuming a poison, one that will kill
Using up all of your staying-still power not firing at will
Slipping and falling like a Victorian mill
Anger eats your insides and makes you ill
Emerging vicious
Cider raising. Glorious.
Leave him in peace inside his new mountain den
His name’s Ben, one of the Portuguese mountain men

Redeeming City Rockers

Redeeming City Rockers
Screaming lechy shockers
Up and down the rails
Telling awful tales

Redeeming City Rockers
You will never stop us
Got that drive for movement
Clear the whole damn room but
Didn't we have a blast?
Oh how we have a laugh
Between Bristol and Bath
And before the second half

Redeeming City Rockers
Love causing a ruckus
Rough edges but dynamic
The Bed Bugs cause you panic

Redeeming City Rockers
Let them try and mock us
Too late we beat you to it
Planted
Sprouted
And grew it
Spew it
All over slacks and shoe it

Gives people a scowl
Beats but not like Howl
I saw the best kinds of penetration
Mutual aid not verbal masturbation
Created by madness
Feeding, satirical, naked
Truth
Strewth
Redeeming City Rockers, uncouth
Like real life
Strife
Meltdown spoof
But proof
There's no doubt
We ain't here to mess about
In a tragic Kingdom
The rhymes we bring them

The content foul
Hood down. No cowl.
Bandanas off faces
Not nice and sweet
Strawberry laces
Fast paces
And perception traces
Down teeming
Disgusting seeming
Front face hidden meaning
Like a horror film screening
Leave you revolted, not beaming

On me you can be leaning
We’re here together dreaming
Ain’t what it’s all seeming
Shake the ceiling

Disaster
Pumping heart
Thumping party
After
Laughter
Wendy Rene
We’ll take any
Shape
Of escape
Plaster peeling

Got that ‘my day’
Friday
Diarrhoea feeling
Everybody’s working for the dead end
Pretend agreeing
Bare bones
Mick Jones
On stage alone
Leave your phone
At home
Tonight's the one

Always penning
So we don't forgetting
Or letting the shit in
That needs correcting
Repetition with loosing meaning
Honest but not demeaning
Help but not intervening
Redeeming City rockers

Up Town Top Skrunting

Up town top Skrunting
Dog on string and trains she’s bunking
Dungarees and chain link clunking
Boots and braces. Polo tucked in.

‘Skrunt’ is a name for a women who's ‘ard
From every single pub she's barred
She don’t take offense if you call her rude
In the nude
You’ll see she got that Tattooed
She wears a Bandana not a snood
She couldn’t care less if you think she’s prude
She ain't impressed if you're some bro dude
Or a punk who writes poetry, crass and crude

Her bars are harsh and fast and ill
She spits them over Bratmobile
Her rhymes are cryptic but you get the gist
She’s got no time for misogynists
She could spark you out that's a given
A monster truck is what's she's driven
Her best life is what she's living
Like many other women
Her journey began
With Kathleen Hannah and Kaitlin Moran

She goes to GAY and she'll go to HEAVEN
She stays up all night 24 L7
Partying hard and misbehaving

Quick left hook and fast mathematics
Hanging around with football fanatics

If you lay hands on her she'll teach you your place
You'll find a grinder boot in your face
If you dare step out of line she'll be on your case
She's a walking talking can of mace

Angels hangout in dirty places
A baseball bat but not running to bases
She always stands up for what's right
And will not take a bar of your shite

She's compassionate and loving though
The kindest person you'll ever know
I'm glad to see that she's around
We need more boots like her on the ground

Cider bottle
Riding on tople
Full throttle
Late copu
Powerful sexually
She can be who she wants to be

If you piss her off then you're out of luck n'
You'll get an earful with a little more chucked in
Dirty jokes she's got a fuck-ton
Smashing out pull ups, feminine hunking
Up town top Skrunting

By @levizerf.tattoo

Came Too Soon

A way to cure the winter gloom
The daily awaiting of the tomb
Tired of dependency
On LSD
Reactions on zoom
Need something brazen
Get your skates on
Quick smart
Click. Start.
In the flesh interaction or two
Maybe I was still thinking about you
Or perhaps I should've gone to the loo

I'm ashamed to say the embarrassment loomed
My spine shivered as we spooned
What a way to kill the mood
Boom-boom-boom
Shake the room
The tension was cut and left to ruin
What the fuck was I thinking or doing
Reached too high then fell to my doom

Ashamed of vulnerability
Closed curtain deniability
'I don't have trouble with that myself mate

A malfunction in which I never partake
Living on the edge, train while you masturbate'
You haven't ever even once?
Just by chance?
Really? Never
Not ever
You're clever
To never
Ever shiver
And quiver

Hand gripped. Blipped and slipped out too sharpish
A burst of air but not quite fartish
Just over the mountain, roll in the…….
"HEY!!
Get a grip and get control
We almost had it! We were on a roll!"
She went and climbed up the wrong pole

Durex vendor, do widzenia
She thought she should
I thought I could
With this wood
Have worked but I stopped the goal
Like Pickford
My dick should
Play professionally
But not if you want me to pleasure thee

One off occasion
It's just a faze n'
Reconnection with the body
Rushing in can get sloppy
Take a moment before you get floppy
And you won't make
The same mistake. Copy.
Pistol at dawn, banging till noon
Don't let yourself feel like a buffoon
Arise again, you're in full bloom
Slipped out. Self-doubt. Came too soon.

Loo of the Year

King's Cross Station
Loo of the year
You won't piss better than that round 'ere
All the other loos quake in fear
You smell them
Before you hear
Then your nose
Tells your eyes
To shed a tear

There's a stool
Pool
On the floor
The pay a grand
To sit or stand tour
In store
For an eyesore
Lock the door
And break the law
Shoes just touching
The piss puddle shore
Clutching
The faeces scrapper
Paper
Crisp as A4
I wanna be adored
Pissed and stoned

Roses
Poses
As Romanic
Frantic
Copulation
Gigantic population
Discreetly
Excreting
In the bog
Standard
No gold medal lanyard
Droplet graveyard
But Kings Cross won
The urinal final
Smart flush
Faster than Usain
Bolt to St. Pants Down
International
The greatest shit-shack in the capital
The finest cubicle
You ever did useical
Don't get it confusical

When your bowels get loosical
Do not give up, no trucicals
Let's not sit
and shit
With the bluesicals
Leg it to King's Cross
The toilet there is boss

If you're at a loss
Join the IT Crowd
Moss
The cool kids hang out in the toilet queue
If you ain't heard the news they'll tell it to you
It's a place to discuss philosophies
And prevent the world's atrocities

We put our differences aside
Don't feel you need to run and hide
It's shit out there, come inside
And glide
Through life
In this 1st class loo
Is there anything else you'd rather do?

The greatest toilet in the land
More shiny than a brass band
Forgot about your dinner plans
Cancel your restaurant reservation
This lav ain't just for masturbation
You could eat off these toilet seats
An all-purpose meet and greet

Your friends and your family
Jump at the offer gladly
More fun than you've ever hadly
Madly
In love with these four walls
When I'm in here I feel 10 ft tall

If you want the greatest time of your life
A place to take the kids and the wife
To find solutions to hate and war
No culture clash no rich and poor
In this place you could want no more
It's a treat for you I’ve got in store
Look no further you’ll find it here
Kings Cross Station Loo of the year

Card Machine Punks

Redeeming Features uses a Card Machine
I know what you think! I agree it's obscene!
It's small and white and shiny and clean
He doesn't even drink or smoke or get lean

That prick RF sells books with cards
What's next? Space shuttles and flying to Mars?
He must be working for the Tzars
In-between screaming and shouting his bars

He thinks he's punk
But he's a flashy cunt
And he accepts debit
I saw him then started a thread on Reddit
Once I knew I couldn't forget it
I had a heart attack! Call a medic!

Redeeming Features uses a Card Reader
Take me to your fucking leader
What is this? A trip to ASDA?
Does he drive a flashy Mazda?

RF thinks he's a high street store
He takes his Card Machine on tour
He doesn't throw enough bottles at the law
What are we discussing this poser for?

If he was real he'd only take speed
With a refund guaranteed
He'd shit up the walls and piss on the floor
He'd steal his pens and note books for sure

Card Machine punks are an embarrassment
I don't want to be arrogant, but look you should
Be causing trouble for the establishment
Not answering to middle management

Don't buy a patch or shirt off this twat
Would you like a receipt with that?

Card Machine Punks
Trading in plastic
The technology has become fantastic
Selling books on Card in the middle of the woods
A Sci-Fi way to trade your goods

Forward reverse flash,
Leftover Chiropract back-crack to the future
Fuck your Card Machine and your computer
Luddites forever keeping it true
I don't wanna change for you
They've all had enough of me
It ain't like Woody Guthrie
That Card Machine doesn't kill fascists
Cause outrage or create panic
Why don't you drink cider and smell like skunks
Card Machine. Card Machine. Card Machine Punks.

Billy the Quid

This is the story of a homeless gent

He don't pay bills or tax or rent
But saves lives
And once rescued some terrified children
From a treacherous burning building…….
He saw it coming like a prophet
The Medway towns never forgot it
They love discussing their favourite topic
Billy the quid, he's always on it

"Have you got a quid mate?"
Is his catch phrase
Alas, Billy didn't used to get much praise
But Billy the quid is more than a man
Who panhandles with his rattling can
Billy the quid is a superhero
When he's not sitting outside Nero

By night he stops atrocities
And goes on life saving Odysseys
Quests to help the old and needy
He spots trouble with his eye so beady
One day on a Chatham afternoon
Bill tapped his coin can with a plastic spoon
To hear the cries of some children nearby
He froze and looked up to the sky

Bill pocketed the cash and jumped to his feet
He left his trusty blanket seat
And ran full pelt to the scene of the crime
He knew that he only had little time
To save the kids and stop the fire
Billy jumped and sprinted but never tired
Weaving in and out of the late night shoppers
Slipping out of the hands of power-mad Coppers

Then Billy made it to the orphanage
He used the gate as some anchorage
And jumped the fence to get inside
If it wasn't for him someone would've died

Out of the window the smoke arose
The soot started filling up Billy's nose
Bill needed access to the main hall
Although he may not be super tall
He's strong like an Ox, and 'ard as stone
He lives and survives and fights alone

A turn on his heel and tension in his core
Bill side-kicked down the front door
1 and 2 and 3 and 4
Times lucky and down it came
In moments like these Billy earned his fame

His Lonsdale T-Shirt went over his mouth
This was life or death, it could all go south
He ran inside with no fear

Billy knew the fire alarm must be near
He smashed his elbow into the glass
Still using his T-Shirt as a mask
Through the smoke and chaos and flames
Bill heard their shouts and found the weans

"Follow me!" he called to the kids
They started to run and make a bid
For freedom. They all made it out of the door.
The locals couldn't believe what they saw
"Thank you Billy, you're the salt of the earth
Tell us, how much is your mission worth?
What do we owe you for your deed so kind?
What price is it that you have in mind?"…

But he's a humble man

…so what Billy did

Was he only asked…

"Have you got a quid?"

Sex Injuries

One too many visits to A and E
Not anarchy and equality
Just X-rays and osteopathy
The only one to blame is me
I got another sex injury

Couldn’t write it
Looked like it
But I wasn't in a fight
It went too far when she pulled out the pincer
Neither of us wanted to seem like a wincer

Aerial antics
Acrobatic
Mid-climax panic
I can't stop. Addicted to the nail dig.
She clawed it, grabbed it
Concussion
Blushing
As we hit the floor
Intact
Impact
Leaves us wanting more

Tooth mark
Shark
Body tours
Like jaws

Took a bite
With all his might
Dislodged coil
They ain't made of tin foil
I had internal bleeding
Loss of feeling
Brutality
Calamity

“Redeeming!
Where did you get that bruise on your thigh?
That chunk out of your neck
And what happened to your eye?”

Scratches
Gashes
Forehead clashes
Someone should have let go
Running amok
Plucked too hard on the banjo
Like playing blue grass
Keith Moon solo
Big bang
Too many teeth, too many teeth per inch
In the wish you hadn't saw arse

The sharp “ping!”
And wincing
From a collision
And ripped incision
Of a nipple ring
Is a painful thing

Hot like kettle
Not in fine fettle
Causing alarma.
Drama.
Dharma.
Karma.
Metal sutra
Threaded through the anus
All gone wrong
Stains on the sheet
I nearly met St. Pete tongue
All over the shlong
Prolonged operation
Swelling-letting like estate agents

Something stuck inside the eye
My oh my American tied up
Wrist chaffing
Ankle breaking
Submerged
Lake
In and out of water
It looks like we fought a

Loch Ness creature
Redeeming Feature
Nail marks on the peach
It's like we had a seizure
But with more pleasure

Whatever the weather
Right now not never
Latex leather or vegan pleather
Untie us, no tether

Burning singeries
Late-night bingeries
Not just a tingeries
Sex injuries

Make Amercia Vomit Again

Big hop
Quick stop
Across the pond
Gun finger
Air linger
Tragic wand
Of disgusting rhymes
I'm rather fond

Verbal diarrhoea
Gnarly
Makes you run quicker
Than white Sheen Charlie
I gather
That MAVA
Is bad for your bladder
Don't listen to RF when you're up a ladder

Revolt spilling out of the end of my pen
Before I blow I'm clucking like a freckled hen
Step into my cavernous disease ridden den
Back in the UK
They like to say
"Donald Trump see you next Tuesday"
Pissing off the far-right since god knows when…

Make America Vomit Again

REDEEMING FEATURES
POETRY
MAKE
AMERICA
VOMIT AGAIN
WEST COAST TOUR 2025

By @_zig_sag

Nazi Poets Do One

Nazi poets do one
Go home and write a new one
Herbert Böhme had his day
Vent your pain some other way
Prejudice and discrimination
Helps you let out your frustration
Trying to book the venue
How long can you pretend you
Always choose a new name
For the same old blame game

Cloak and dagger
Grifter. Blagger.
British moving
Unamusing
Punching down, low blows
Spreading filth like Goebbels
Always in and out of the clink
You need to find yourself a shrink

I feel pure pity
Dreamed up purity
Stemmed from rejection
Insecurity
Projection
Like magic lantern
Scapegoat. Phantom.

Torch. Pick.
Cheap trick

You want us to want you
None of what you say is true
Propaganda. Stage and screen. Dramatic.
Stirring up division and panic

Sort your life out, start again
Redemption and correction
But I'm afraid until then
Nazi poets do one
You ain't got a clue son
Your battle is a long one
Because it will never be won
March into the ocean
We know that you're a wrong'un

'Tomorrow belongs to…' who the fuck are you?
Strength through boy
Stuck in the dole queue
They only come to adopt your view
When they have nowhere else to run to
You've got a nasty poison tongue
Nazi poets do one

Creatine Made Me Shit Myself

Creatine made me shit myself
Creatine gave me the runs
I should write a poem about it
Imagine the Creatine puns

Creatine made me cack and shout
Shit falling out of my bum
I thought I'd be fine but sadly
Creatine gave me a dodgy tum

Maybe it's not good for your healthia
Like 'Always Sunny in Philadelphia'
I couldn't take it back
To the shop either

Rancid like 'Let's Go',
Thunder guts. Oh no,
Flushed it down
The brown
Liquid smeared
Over engineered
Body rehab
Soiling red flag
Agg
Big strength gain
With rectal pain
Creatine gave my arse a drain

Amino acid
The side effect man is a bastard
Like gastric enteritis
Not the nicest
Better think twice
It gets you strong
Means you can go on
Long
With your workout

But I forgot about
The warning
That morning
As I loaded up the shaker
Risk taker
Bowel breaker
Anti-agent caker
Sphincter earth quakka
Better off with oats
Wouldn't happen to goats
They'll eat whatever
They want
And chomp all day
Without their arse giving way

Gory details
Self-scorning
No glory
Entrails
Hold it in fails

I blurted, when it spurted out
Horrified about
How it hit me in the foot
A yellow look
To the substance
In abundance

Last chance
Too much capacity
I got the poo fear
Sheer
Rectal tenacity
And the Sundance
Bid for freedom
A summer's day spent on the loo
And cleaning up liquid poo
I wish I could tell you it wasn't true
But then I would be lying to you

My argument
Against the supplement
Is that it wasn't worth the time I spent
Wiping off splatters from my leg
Stains go crusty like Lister of Smeg

Ducking
Chucking
Inward sucking
Oh no! Fucking hell!
Fell

From heaven
Stairway to 7-Eleven
Coz I ran out of roll
This stuff took my dignity and my soul

Creatine made me shit myself
I stood there in shock
Once the seal was broken
No I couldn't fucking stop

In an attempt to improve my health
I took some powder off the shelf
Pencil rolling toilet stealth
Creatine made me shit myself

Fuck Off Redeeming Features

If this poem has a trigger warning, then what the fuck was that?
If that one didn't have a trigger warning, then where the fuck are we at?
This headcase is shouting again his oral assault is back
I feel like I'm under audio, verbal and lyrical attack

Someone get this man off the stage, this bloke is a fucking nut
He's going to say something awful again, I can feel it in my gut
Someone stop Redeeming Features before he shouts again
This man is a fucking loon he should be locked up in the pen

Redeeming Features shrieks and yells, the man is fucking obscene
Redeeming Features we want him to fuck off back to where he's been
I came out for a poetry night and this man is shouting at me
I want to hear poems about nice things so fuck off and let me be

Get Redeeming Features off the stage he's kicking off again

He promised he'd stop shouting but he didn't tell us
when
Redeeming Features causing chaos and mayhem since
day
He could redeem his features by just fucking going away

www.ingramcontent.com/pod-product-compliance
Lightning Source LLC
LaVergne TN
LVHW020049110826
845155LV00029B/703

* 9 7 8 1 9 1 1 2 3 2 6 2 9 *